A HISTORY OF KINDNESS

A HISTORY OF KINDNESS

poems

Linda Hogan

TORREY HOUSE PRESS

SALT LAKE CITY • TORREY

The author is grateful to the following journals and anthologies for publishing some of the poems found in this book: *World Literature Today, Cimarron Review, Poetry, Pembroke, Split This Rock, The Eloquent Body, Cutthroat, StorySouth, Thinking Continental, Red Leaf Poetry, Ghost Fishing, Yellow Medicine Review, About Place Journal, Oklahoma Today, Emergence Magazine, Canadian Review of Comparative Literature, Beacon, The Radiant Lives of Animals, Poesia Indigena, Ecopoetry, ISLE.*

First Torrey House Press Edition, April 2020
Copyright © 2020 by Linda Hogan

Published by Torrey House Press
Salt Lake City, Utah
www.torreyhouse.org

International Standard Book Number: 978-1-948814-25-6
E-book ISBN: 978-1-948814-26-3
Library of Congress Control Number: 2019952010

Cover design by Kathleen Metcalf
Interior design by Rachel Davis
Distributed to the trade by Consortium Book Sales and Distribution

Torrey House Press offices in Salt Lake City sit on the homelands of Ute, Goshute, Shoshone, and Paiute nations. Offices in Torrey are in homelands of Paiute, Ute, and Navajo nations.

MIX
Paper | Supporting
responsible forestry
FSC
www.fsc.org   FSC® C008955

For Kyan Red Star and Kayse Red Star

Contents

Book One

The Body Life

The Red Part

When I was a girl
the old women told me if I were always generous
I could paint a part in the middle of my hair with red.
Red ochre. Red paint. Red lipstick some even used.
But it seemed not right
to reveal to the world
that I was generous,
as if the announcement takes it back.
So, unlike other girls,
I appeared selfish
even if I gave so much away.
Who would have known
I gave my buckskin dress, my leggings
and moccasins, beaded so well,
even the silver bands for my hair.

I think of the many red parts,
even the parting of the sea
by Moses leading his people
in a never-ending story,
or the parting in the red stem
of the plant for healing bad lungs,
the splitting of the heart
when one side works against the other
and the veins in their miles
flow back again and again.

But the red part I recall the most
had to do with generosity, and then
our giving up the taken land and forest
to those who wanted it so.
We parted with our clothing,
our families, and on our way
we left the red farewell
of a blood trail along the land
we walked,
writing that became
the book coming after us
with words of truth.

When the Body

When the body wishes to speak, she will
reach into the night and pull back the rapture of this growing root
which has no faith in the other planets of the universe,
but her feet have walked in the same bones
of the ancestors over long trails,
leaving behind the oldest forest. They walk on the ghosts
of all that has gone before them, not just plant, but animal, human,
the bones of the ones who left their horses to drink with them
at the spring running through earth's mortal body
which has much to tell about what happened that day.

When the body wishes to speak from the hands, it tells
how it pulled children back from death and it remembers every detail,
washing the children's bodies, legs, bellies, the delicate lips of the girl,
the vulnerable testicles of the son,
that future my people brought out of the river
in a spring freeze. That is only part of the story of hands
that touched our future.

This all started so simply, just a body with so much to say,
one with the hum of her own life in a quiet room,
one of the root growing, finding a way through stone,
one not remembering nights with men and guns,
the ragged clothing and broken bones of my body.

Let's go back to the hands, the thumb that makes us human,
but don't other creatures use tools and lift what they need,
intelligent all, like the crows here, one making a cast of earth clay
for the broken wing of the other, remaining
until it healed, then breaking the clay to fly away together.

I would do that, too,
since a human can make no claims
better than any other, especially without wings,
only hands that don't know these intelligent lessons.

Still, I think of the willows
made into a fence and even cut, they began to root and leaf,
then tore off the wires as they grew.

A human does throw off the bonds if she can, if she tries, if it's possible.
The body is so finely a miracle of its own, created of the elements
of anything that lived on earth
where everything that was
still is.

Bathing with Tender Care

And not this time the body of my child,
but my own skin, loving the wrinkled knees
and the scars dealt the child I was,
loving the skin between toes,
how soft, verily soft,
like the tenderness
behind the knees.
How could I have so disliked this body
in my life, the one water so laves
in the small tub of a warm storm's tides.
Just like the other women I know,
the girls, so interrupted by our own proportions
to the world of ought.
I look at the picture of my grandmother;
never was there a lapse of my love
for the larger fit of her flesh,
only for her sweetness, her kindness.
And great grandmother, no teeth but a smile,
she sits on the stump of a once large tree,
that enthrones her wide hips.
Tobacco chewing, pipe smoking, snuff inhaling women,
these, and my great great grandmother,
the picture from a newspaper all I have of her
except something inside me that is
what she is, except she looked so stern. Maybe
it is the hunger times, or maybe,
god forbid, a part of me,
but I like her dark darkness, the bone earrings,
hair pulled back straight and black.

Did they feel about themselves
as women today or did they merely think
I have grown, I have grown older?
Never will I not love
this skin which is created of those women.
Never will I not bathe slowly, washing
my elbows, that dent beneath my arm,
the cleft between my legs,
the belly still so gently soft,
all the skin so once tight
but loosening now
as if there is more, much more
room for life,
for this body,
more love to live inside
the beauty I have become
made flesh,
warmer now than the water.

About Myself

I come from a land once plenty.
I came from the caves of a world,
and tall grasses
where earth rises and falls
as the ribs of a body,
bones all in their hiding,
but also as water rises and falls
like breath with salt water tides
following the phases of moon.
Yet the human signs are here
in this two-legged animal,
imperfectly woven
but twined well enough
to be a burden basket
filled with the gatherings
of today's work,
returning home
with a common hunger,
but about myself, I am
merely one brief living shine.

Lost in the Milky Way

Some of us are like trees that grow with a spiral grain
as if already prepared for the path of the spirit's journey
to the world of all souls.

It is not an easy path.
A dog stands at the opening constellation
before you can reach the great helping hand.

The dog wants to know,
did you ever harm an animal, hurt any creature
or take a life you didn't eat?

This is only the first of our cosmic maps. There is another
my people made of what is farther
beyond this galaxy.

It is a world that can't be imagined by usual means.
After the first,
it could be a map of forever.

It is a cartography
shining only at certain times of the year
like a great web of finery

some spider pulled from herself
to help you recall your true following,
your first breath in the dark cold.

The next door opens and Old Woman
counts your scars. She is interested in how you have been
hurt and not in anything akin to sin.

From between stars are the words we now refuse;
loneliness, longing, whatever suffering
might follow your life into the sky.

Once those are gone, the life you had
against your own will, the hope, even the prayers
take you one more bend around that river of sky.

What We Kept

We had mountains
and you took down the trees
so that rain felled the mountains.

It was once enchanted
with the song of golden winds,
the silk thread of river,
pollen from the medicine flowers
you took. The whole world
was the gold you wanted.

In the past, we gave you our labor.
We gave you our store of food,
even the mats where you slept for a year
before we sent you away with burning arrows
and your fat ran across earth.

You took the plants
from our beautiful woods
on your ships
to lands already destroyed,
and even more of you arrived
to take our homes
while we still lived inside them.

You took the birds
from the rookeries of beautiful waters,
feathers for hats from near the mangroves,
coats made from our animals,
and all the time
you lost so much, even taking,

because you knew so little
that a girl led the way
to the fame of men,
fed them, turned their canoes
to safety.

The more you took,
the more you lost.
And you need us now
the way
you needed us then, our land
and labor,
and we give to you
knowledge you don't hear,
the new mind you can't accept,
our bone and leaf soup.

But what I keep
to myself,
for myself, is the soul
you can never have
that belongs to this land,
the magic haunting you
still and always untaken,
but you want,
how you want,
how you need.

Recuerdo

Let me take it through my heart again,
that unchanging moment,
you wading through the river,
me wading toward you, laughing,
the illumination of that moment,
the shine of our skin,
the clouds coming toward us,
the sky beings who live above
with tears ready to fall
like the origins of rain; no one knows
what they have seen in their previous fluid form.

For now, I merely go through that one day again,
remembering, traveling toward the river
past the place where snakes shed their skin
against stone and move on
new, shining like a constant,
ceaseless stream of water
as it crawls across earth changing and passes
blood memory, salt water memory,
toward our laughter and joy
that moves once again through this heart.

The Feet and Where They Travel

Let me start with my feet. One holds a curved and graceful
line for the loving artist's eye to follow, a warm hand to touch.
I remember its life, dancer on ice, youthful bodily happiness,
kissed by the lover; wishing all had been only this morning.

The knee remembers the fortunes of poor landings.
It had to settle for this woman it has carried
from black-haired infant kicking and laughing with joy,
to the tree-climbing, branch-sitting
child of forest, to the watcher of her own children.

And the hips also went along with that small-boned
girl to her child-carrying womanhood.
That's when the body was so easily forgotten.
It became fallen into armies of war, a history of that larger
body politic that took away a father, a love, broke my family.

The world takes a bit at a time. It takes
what it wants by pain, injury, hunger, war.

On the subject of war; some are refugees
all hoping to survive
their lives walking across earth, carried on a cot or inner tube.

I am merely one woman carried still by my own feet
of necessity, one still healthy,
the other broken, but strong enough for this journey
of what has become someone else's
country by taking, by theft, and this exiled body
living in time with a multitude of other travelers.

Lies About the Body

Window on the south.
Window on the east,
along there is where I tell the lies,
that everything is fine
after I fell down how many times.
Yes, I am well
though pain overtakes my bones
from the foot when I rise like the glorious sun
having forgotten overnight
I am not able to move, to walk,
this body, some lost grace
that moves like the great cat,
an arrow through the bones
pretending it will escape
or even worse,
escape.

Down from the Sky

1.

If you sleep with a rock for a pillow
you may see the same ladder
Jacob saw, climbing a dark night.
Now people of all countries
want to reach that sky they call heaven,
but they fall back to earth,
the dust and ash of their ancestors.

I ask, why the sky
when below is such great company,
the turtle and water spider, the deer,
and the great serpent mound my ancestors created.

So dislodge the rock your poor head slept on
and look beneath, at the lace of roots,
the red and pale threads passing through,
worms that create good earth for your corn and squash.
This is the path,
where each thing begins from seed,
or an insect egg opens its sac
and some blue-winged beauty emerges.

2.

I live here in the forest.
I try to warm myself with wood from broken earth,
thankful to look out on this tribal land
where we were the nightmares of others,
savages of spiritual wisdom
come from dreamers and those who prayed
to makers, to creators, to earth mothers and to water
in different languages,
speaking, hoping with such intelligent words
this world would never fall.
Just think, what we did rise from, after all,
how reach this place to begin
and how I do find it
still whole.

Bone, Looking at the Pieta

Mineral; it is not the same as a human life.
The quarry, not only the hunt for a hold on one man's life.
Dolomite, not just the pale chain of mountains,
>>*but many words, these have become the transformation of stone into*
>>>*pain,*
pain to stone.
>>*Calcite. Matrix, the near-human veins of color unearthed from a*
>>>*mine.*

Calcium, weren't you milk
like the marble statue of a simple mother with her son
grown, loved, in this last moment laid across her legs
as forever she weeps, having lifted him to her,
she so small, he so large. Lifted,
he reached too high, so kindly they say,
as if it is not in us all,
that kind bone,
the mineral bone of humanity,
the one that bent
to wash the feet of the poor
in the light of every day.
Feet have many small bones.
His walked countless lands,
the heat of a desert, some say even the water,
feet fitting themselves, this permanent moment
into the wrong pierced sandal of flesh
barely and forever held in the lap of the mother.

If Home Is the Body

If, as they say, your home resembles your body,
please pardon my rumpled clothing,
this untidy appearance. But in this home
are pockets of memory,
stones I carried from places of holiness,
beside disordered papers, so plentiful and unfinished.

The windows need no curtains.
Only light peers in
as does the moon from the black
vessel of night rising over red mountains.
I think how the nautilus rises,
shining on the surface of every darkness.

The house is old with dusty corners
where memories have settled
along with my gifts from deep oceans.

Inside, a picture of two women
ride through a red valley on horses.
A Woodlands family smiles,
the child standing proud beside his father
and the kindness and love of the mother.
Rarely do you see us in photos this way, so happy.

In one corner hangs a strand of blue beads from Turkey
to protect, as do lucky coins,
tree frogs climbing the window
to sing before rain,
and the sounds of crickets.

Last is the dog with her wet paws.
She loves each morning, going out,
leaving the house,
returning to announce,
I am here.

The Fingers, Writing

Not all fingers hold a nail
waiting for the hammer.
Not all take up white thread
and transform it to lace.
Even fewer pick up the pen
and offer words to a lover's
body where it is so beautifully dark
as we lay in the sunlit field of grasses,
wildflowers, olive trees,
a gathering of life.

The hands have their reasons
unknown to the heart,
a needed touch,
the kindness of another skin.

The fingers have their own aims,
to make beauty, to touch softly
something to live by.

But then I remember that sometimes they lie
when from out of the dark corridors
of some mind
they sign a writ of death.

I remember the musician who had his fingers broken
for creating songs his country didn't want.
The same is true for other lands.

As for my people, a government of hands
entreat for their land, pen and ink like blood
wrote away each stand
of ancient forest, the waters
we drank gone with the grand larceny
of fingers holding nothing
but a pen and a bottle of ink,
our stolen indigo, dark as blood.

In the distance between hand and soul
lies the history of this continent.
So now I write this poem.
Some of us have to tell
what has been done,
what they will do
now, even tomorrow,
the truth of what happens.

Bones at the River

When the river changed course
and washed land away,
each bend grew sharper.

Water takes what it wants.
This time, it says, I will take
earth from where your people
are buried.

The river was once far from our graveyard
but this Washita changed course,
stole earth and carried it
on the snaking back of its current.
Now it passes through
the place my people are buried.

We are those
who came from the ones
who survived, buried in that place
after walking the death trail
from Mississippi. *Missa Sipokna.*

We walked into this lost foreign place
having no home,
no body of peace,
just the papers
with signatures
of those who made promises not held.

Now our bones are revealed like truth.
We've taken up two
from once invisible lives,
lost names, lost horses,
our lost relations
who would have loved us.
From some other place they do.

And I think what they feel in that force of water.
We lived and traveled by water.
It was our life. So I say to our bones, *Yes, go!*

Creation

I am a warrior
wanting this world to survive
never forgotten, this earth
which gave birth to the bison, the scissortail,
the vultures of Tibet who consume the finally released
mystics like my own old ones
who taught that we are always a breath,
a breath away from bullets.

I am from a line of songs,
a piece of history told by our people.
In every gully lies the power of a forest song waiting to begin,
the first ones sang when they crossed into this existence
and down to the canyon where I live.
I dreamed they passed
the creek-bed, each canyon wall,
the stones I love, lichens growing on them,
the route I go to the river where bear also fish.

It is hard for some to know
the world is a living being.
They live with forgotten truth
replaced with belief. Perhaps that's why
the books of the Mayans were burned,
and written languages destroyed in the North.

You can weep over such things
as lost love, or the passing of loved ones,
but always remember those birds, the bison,
their grief, too, and how the land hurts
in more chambers than one small heart
may ever hold.

The Maps

When I went to the return of our ancestors
to the dozed open earthen mounds,
the bones were wrapped in white, all clean
as if held in dry caves on a ledge.
In the same place they were found,
they are returned.

I think of true history,
our saved seeds, sumpweed, grasses for attracting deer,
an older order of corn than we know.
But we know that place in our blood.
We knew where the three gods
were dug from a mound of earth: A man. A woman. A bear.
Documented, then taken by the French and never seen by us again.

Strange, but the bill of an ivory billed woodpecker was found
over the hill from where I now live
in a small burial mound.
They believe it was traded, the ivory bill of one who once flew
plentiful across the southern line,
now gone, overtaken like the pigeons that flew in dark clouds
across the meeting of rivers near Cahokia, the city before cities
where journeys ended from waterways and trails are marked
on stone walls along the river,
trees bent to show the way.

Consider how the world has changed
from what it would have been
if the beaver had been left alone
to make the meadows and the river
both with their own ways of coursing through land,
changing it to their will, not ours.

Consider the map if we had used the seed saved in the dry cave,
the bones of what it would have been, all of it,
mounds shaped like eagles, turtles, the water spider,
or how light still enters one side
to walk toward a great bowl of water, every eighteen years,
where sky watchers know what stars tell others
and where the milky way takes us back
to the fold of the galaxy, a spiral trail souls follow
when they walk away from the body rib.

Skin

It's the largest organ of the body and I wish
I could tell you what it was to lose so much of it
when being dragged until I was only blood
and the thin nerves of this body where one pain ends
and another begins far from where it started,
just like the underground strands of communication
from tree to tree.

Bark, when I see you with an injury
and the amber colored sap like golden blood,
I have to wonder if nerves are inside,
if it hurts the same. I can't help
but to bandage you.

The Pine Forest Calls Me

I remember how it has grown these years.
Yet the spring pinecones are still young,
soft and gentle as skin to the touch.
It is always the green season here, even with future amber
formed golden from bark
with the scent of animal life that passed through.
If a traveler should pass by, it summons,
Stop, come in, stay.

I remember one poet taking a branch of pine
from the winter forest to his dying sister.
It was all she wanted in her last moment.
I have never forgotten the snow dripping
from that branch to the floor.

It is what I want, too,
not so much to have a branch taken away,
but for myself to be taken to this world
my own life passed through
as it does now in the shadows
where sun filters in
to melt snow, quench earth,
that water dripping from trees.

You smell it, too, so let's remain a while in its shade.
How I love this forest,
where the hieroglyphs of insects
work the inner layers of bark
like monks writing unseen in deep silence,
and if you know the true secret of falling
you might summon that magic language.

I know prayers rise with smoke
the way some people
are so perfectly uplifted
from their first roots.
But when this life of trying is finally over,
bring to my bed a small branch
smelling of green forest,
the melting pure water of snow,
these mysteries discovered
one more time.

Nativity

Of the bloods I come from,
how they loved the salt water of the womb,
of oceans
of memory not one I ever forget.
Yesterday is still today
in our history. We speak of the past
in present tense because it is
that skin close, blood and fingernail scratch close.

I know the forests south of here,
how we pounded
hickory nuts into sweet cream
then rolled it up in hide,
and traded for copper and dried buffalo.

Now I am too many treaties to read,
all the rivers engineers moved,
the land behind the dam.
I am the artifacts
drowned in water.
In the time one body left
another arrived.
My hands labored with the young,
the earth, our horse people,
respecting hoof, mane, eyes
and watching where the ears turn to listen.

This is how much a body can hold
within the organ called skin, even now,
and I am not yet the end of our line.

Embodied

I am embodied first by the numbers
given my grandparents
as, trembling, they signed the Dawes Act.

Outside under the moving night sky
I wonder
what it is to be made of this continent
from the beginning.
I came from the salt and water of those before me
before the creation of zero,
and then those numbers given my grandparents
by the American government
and names that belonged to others.
The past we have not forgotten.
They said you only pass on the people's story
by telling it. You keep it by giving
it away. So I do.

For children of this land,
yesterday is close as today.
It's why I know the forest south of here,
hickory cream and seeds for trade.
I labor daily here with the other descendants
of the pyramid builders of this continent,
pyramids greater than those of Egypt
and unknown, some already destroyed,
by the Americans.

I am one of the Indian Horse people
alive since the last standing treaty.
We are not yet the end of this line.
I am not yet the end of their plans.
And still the standing equines
hiding in the rich forest, swimming our rivers,
all so alive they breathe
for us, and two share the love,
embodied this way, water and blood,
knowledge passing between.

Once I was told you become what you think
so I think the gone animals back,
the ivory billed woodpecker,
the river of sharp teeth,
swimming black turtles shining,
all that fell
from this life I name Whole.

Book Two

Old Mother

Eagle Feather Prayer

I thank the eagle and Old Mother for this prayer
I send to earth and sky
and to the sacred waters.

I thank Old Mother and the golden eagle.
They are the ones who taught me to pray
with no words. They taught the part of me
that is unnamed by anatomy books
and so I stand here
facing you and the rest of creation
also with secret names.
I send this prayer thanking those who risk their lives
for clean, sweet water,
and once again there is the great silence
of what happened to the buffalo
and so hard it is to pray for the shooters
who laughed about hitting the girl
with one good shot.

We love our horses. We love the dogs who helped us.
We love the wilderness of buffalo herds.
We are humans
who love,
but I don't know what they are,
the shooters,
or their purpose for being.

With no words, just part of my named self
I hold this fan from Old Mother and the eagle.
With all my strength, I send this prayer
so very silent.

We Have Walked Down Past

We have walked down past
the bison who has matured into darkness
and it seems she is a day that passed.
We have walked past the house of bones
left by the mountain lion round this curve of land,
the den of snakes by the fallen large stones
and the place water rises from earth.
I think the mountain lion left the buffalo calf alone
knowing she was holy
and others left prayer flags on the trees,
tobacco ties, each with heart.
It was the flood place of twenty-thirteen.
The path washed away and Old Mother
has no easy walking, her arm holding mine
until we find the right walking stick.
Then solid is her step as we go to the cave
changed since the flood,
water still leaving
a pile of pine needles and twigs carried by the deluge
but new flowers blooming.
After the rain, pollen washed gold to earth
and Old Mother gathers it like a bee
into her bag. She uses it to heal,
pray, for her conversations
with the water and the sky,
the clouds and the bison.

Walking by Stolen Creek

The meaning of its name forgotten,
the word remembered.
Whatever happened here
is recalled
in another time and it's remembered
inside the stolen self
that my blood river passes through
in thin and beautiful veins, not gold
but only a mere human heartbeat,
a circle of people
standing, talking, making their plans
as water passes by.
Something, someone is still alive, telling.
They think these are only stories
not what holds the world together
in its balance.

Buffalo Road: Leaving South Dakota

Here are the ridges buffalo made in the hillsides.

In some land it would be an arroyo
or the long brush of wind carving stone
with its strong breath in time
as it parts the grasses.

Each element had its time here,
gun metal, powder, water,
dark shadows of late afternoon,
wild horses concealed in those shadows
and the cold thinking of snow
or red sun
peeling the barns like burned skin.

And then the snow-filled hoof,
the horns,
the chins with dark tufts,
matted wool forced to the forest
to stand with the minus,
the many horses lying
with red shadows of dusk
and blood.

Even Miles
and Custer tried
to subtract this world,
to take any living thing,
even the newly born,
from the numbers of human and creature life,

to the food, body, hoof, claw,
the ghost animals,
driving them away from earth,
the killing of horses,
massacre of bison,
and that was never enough.

Gods, let us be those
who create, give, make,
and do not ever take
more than we offer

here in this broken down
shadowed heart and tongue of the world
in the surprise of stone that says
Something great passed through here,
through the dark bluffs,
the dark fur of earth skin,
life with its large purpose
long before the gathered hay
that now sits gold at the fence line.

The underground roots
remember the sound of each beat
that ran through,
each pounding run,
each spill of blood
that parted the world.

Old Mother

Sitting on the large stone Old Mother says,
I feel it breathing. And it is, as if she opened
the world life where everything does
breathe like the waves of far ocean
taking in air, giving out the cloud waters
passing over us right now.
The bison breathed this air, she says,
and people from other nations.
Don't you hear it
all singing, even the stars above
hidden by daylight, the waters beneath us,
and the first cry of your children when they arrive
from the birth waters to air.
She is the one
showing a way
as she points her feather.
Every path is right, she says. It matters
not which one you follow, just breathe and sing
as you pass along, loving every other traveler.

That Stone from the River

This stone tells the story of what happened here
when people came from the four directions more than a hundred years ago
to talk about who lived on this land and this water.
The earth and stone are still singing the same as before.
They are telling another story about forests killed for dark corporations,
shipping America to other continents,
sending oil from between tectonic plates,
the dark earth that needs to be held in shape.
If only someone thought how everything moves
beneath their feet. If only they saw the fish
with tumors and bleeding scales, born the wrong way,
and the Tar Sand people in pain, the lungs of children
who cannot breathe
so now the winds are singing
the terrible ballad of water:
Ft. Union. Thunder Creek. Lost Creek. Medicine Bow.
Muddy Creek. Missouri. Animas.
Flint River. This stone, all this
revealed.

The Buffalo Again

This morning I woke to find the buffalo out behind the horses.
It was eating the longer blades of grass. I worried about blades.
I worried about its tongue. Then I thought it wanted to speak.
Old Mother believed it wanted to tell us
about the long great

absence

the silence.

The Names of Creeks

Old Woman Creek.
One Dog Creek.
Dead Horse Creek.
It makes a person wonder what happened there,

but Sand Creek we remember
and we'd like to go back
to long before it happened
and turn time around
instead of people.

Before I was born
the plans for killing were made
down the hill from where I live
at Bear Creek as it moves through here,
thank god.

Col. Chivington was present
with other men
with no compassion
in their hearts
as they made plans against the nations
they said they called Friends.

Power eats the world.
It swallows the waters
that come out of earth.

The desire for it is hate, not creation
the way they say love
or friendship may be ordained
in its dark shadow,
its ominous decisions
of blood
and fallen bodies.

Their power swallows wilderness.
It shoots elders, children, mothers,
then takes their memory and changes the story
for those of us who want the truth,
of stories that hold our world together
or show the fault lines of history.

Still it haunts me now that I know
from here came that ominous decision
of blood and fallen bodies
from the dark hate
and hunger, the desire for land
and copper the white men wanted.

The old ones knew true riches;
each plant, each stone, all the creeks,
human tributaries,
the story of what transpired
in every place,
and now what has happened there.

Remember that speaking stone
the boy walked past. He heard it
tell the many things that happened
then taught him how to continue.

When an old woman was sick, he said,
one plant shone above others in the field.

But another power swallows us now.
It steals hearts and souls. Then more.
It steals the mind. My friend said of our present lives,
a mind is a terrible thing to steal.

The Mountain Between

Down at Bear Creek
running through our town
is where the Sand Creek Massacre
was planned.
From down there, up the mountain
and down into a valley
is the hidden little cabin where I live.
Old Mother closed her eyes
when I learned this.
She said, Good thing there is a mountain
between you and those words.

A Need for Happiness

The buffalo in the back field is covered with clumps of snow,
fur thick, knotted with small twigs,
gnarls of darkness
and heavy skin I can't divine
where she came from
but Old Mother says
she crossed over
Highway 70 from where Buffalo Bill
was buried the next hill over,
leaving the herd.

Do you remember him and his show? Red Cloud was there.
Now it's the name of the school where your baby went.
My girl, she said, you need
to understand time and how it travels.
They did, those crossing space to other countries,
the broken, beautiful warriors all still
except Bill. What had he done in this world
but starve people and kill,
and here we are across time
when he killed the most buffalo;
that was his fame,
and even with none nearby
this one is here
away from the herd.

Those great leaders, even with grief,
they laughed together at night
when the light-bearded man left.
They talked and laughed together.

They still loved life,
so why don't you?

Outside My Cabin

The day the buffalo appeared
where I live with wild horses,
I thought, They are clearing the land again
for ranches,
after the old growth, as they did
clear us away,
then the wild horses,
and even the wolves.

Recently a pack of wolves came down
from the Yellowstone fire,
five ghostly presences floating
across the snow.
No one believed me at first
and that was good
because no shooters saw them here.

It was as if they were transparent,
but the ghostly animals killed a deer
outside my window.
I followed the blood,
a thinning trail to the pink, chewed bones,
only teeth marks still on them.

Later I returned from work
to find they'd attacked an elk.
When I stepped forward
they disappeared so quickly
into the wind-blown snow
but the still living elk remained close
with the horses
until it healed.
I was its protector.
Then it was gone.

I tell no one
about the buffalo
living here now
because I know what they would do.
You ask why would they do it.
I think it is in their blood
to leave a forest of cleared trees
a wake of red,
as if they can
or can't
help themselves.

Old Mother Remembers

Old Mother says she remembers when the near city
was a buffalo wallow.
How hard to imagine such large bodies
with legs in air, backs loving the earth,
and keeping their temperature to lesser heat.
She remembers when the long grasses fed them.
She looks outside at the one that is behind the wild horse
and says, Just think how much memory is in that body,
how much memory resides in every cell,
some of it happiness to run with others through the grass,
some of it seeing what happened before
and so miserable that it carries that memory.

Memory

From the spoken memory of some ancestors
we were people of inner earth
who came to this world through caves shining with crystal.

Other people arrived when their first mother
fell through a hole in the sky.

Some climbed a reed into this world.

Others followed starlight.

According to their book,
some were the result of the words, Let there be, Selah.
Three words stood them into existence.

In this flood of immigration,
we now occupy the same precious earth and time.
Who knows if we might ever find our way to another,
and so we live according to the rules laid down at the beginning
like song lines, dreamtime, our laws have great devotion
with respect to this creation.

After our own people climbed through the damp caverns
we dwelt on a ledge above the river of life
in homes with roofs they said were embedded with shining pearls,
gifts from that river wc called The Long Person.

Much time has passed since then, so we almost forgot that earlier one.
Wars came and went. Spanish, British, French, Americans.

I think all this while I am stopped,
waiting for an old turtle to cross the road.
She carries her known past
in the amazing design of shell,
the claws, a being all whole and unbroken,
She is so old the moss grows on her back.
All this while in the distance of waiting.

Watching Over

This land, I watch over it,
the place with ancient stories,
the plants of medicine,
the place where mountain lions
walk down the hill and look in on the light of my life

in this little cabin made of happiness,
of stone laid on stone so perfectly
a hundred years ago,
the year before my father was born.

People came from afar just to see
that new Indian baby, all silent
in his presence, the way we did live
then with the newly born.

The bison is now down in the valley
filled with great trees,
down near the quartz shining
in veins through dark earth.

The fireplace is made of that quartz,
some with crystals bright in firelight,
and pushed into the mortar, the single baby tooth
of the one new child.

In this valley of trees and river and crystal,
the fault lines of history broke.
Now something always watches over
this small cabin, the bison away from its herd,

the ghostly wolves that passed
outside the door last year,
the great hawk flying across
and even the fox that sits each morning

and looks in for no other reason
than to watch how I live,
to make sure it is
the right way.

We Used to Have Pearls

I once asked Old Mother what became of the pearls
that decorated our oldest roofs.

She said the Spanish stole them in bags too heavy
to carry. Some of our pearls spilled over.

But in truth it was their own souls they carried.
No longer did they shine.

When your spirit no longer shines,
you crave gems.

They wore too much armor
even in the heat.

Old Mother said once your spirit fears the world
that world is broken.

That's when you create something to shield you
from imagined harm.

I think of them dragging our shining pearls
and remember they lived in armor.

Imagine the bodies inside it.

Holly Springs, Mississippi

It was night when I walked into the deep cool forest
the dry autumn leaves
at the place my ancestors were sent away
from land they loved so long they'd become it.

They were being sent into the hunger place.
Old Mother knew this was where they camped
the night before they left on their way to becoming bones.

Out behind the trees
a great light burned and I saw fires
the men built just before this one more loss.

They must have grieved as they rode about with torches
deciding who would leave first,
the strong or the weak?

And who would help the infirm, the elders,
as they began that journey to death or new life?
When smoke and firelight disappeared, I knew this was a vision.

I am not one for visions.
It is that they must happen in dark forests
with the shadows of early ancestors holding the fire.

When the old world leaks through
it is never something I could have known
in a book or a story,

just the bright firelight between trees
of our old world
was what it took, and the next day
I read about the fire and how it began,
not a town there, but by the torchlight of one grieving man.

Distance Not Time

I am just wishing to take life up from the earth
to make this my own living
not by the hour, the month, or year.
I don't want to live by time,
but by acre, mile, or maybe the mist stretched over a lake
early one morning in the mountains.
I want to be more than one brief life
that will become frail, but rather a journey
over plains, glaciers, and oceans,
with people whose language
has no past tense, so we forgive
and continue to tell happy stories
of where we have traveled
beyond this place.

But before I am able to tell this to children
a spring breeze comes from far
through the open window
carrying the smell of sage and sweet grass.

So now I need you to know the mystery,
that neither of these grow here,
not in this place.

Book Three

The Radiant Field

God of the Prairies

What name is the god of the prairies,
in this place so large and humble, so filled with medicines
and even the tunneling creatures of earth being
the ones who call down rain.

Beneath this richness are rivers, a lake underneath.
Children, that water below was what I wished for you,
more water than remains,
here where no one of us is superior
to the minions of insects, the butterflies
coming to the plants,
the wealth of wings,
and at the golden march, the flash of red.

I was born to this,
singing or telling a story to tall grasses,
the horses, alive and listening as they are,
and evening hearing the past dark thunder
of bison running down the distance
fighting back their hooves.

This land is honest, at least,
and the other creatures never lie,
all those many gods of the prairie,
here, in this place, and the stand of trees
down near the river, trees not yet cut,
so no drought there,
not yet.

One Creation

I am a warrior
wanting this world to survive
never forgotten, this earth
which gave birth to the bison, the scissortail
the vultures of Tibet consuming the finally released
mystics, the old ones
who taught we are always a breath
away from bullets.

I am from a line of songs,
a particle of history told by the wrong people,
a country before lines of division.
In every gully lies the power of a forest waiting.
It heard the stories the elders told when they crossed
this canyon where I live. I dreamed they passed down
to the creek-bed, each human creation still present,
also loving the same stones I love, the mosses between them,
the remembered creek that runs all year.

It is hard for some to know
the world is a living being.
Some live with forgotten truth.
Others replaced truth with belief.
That's why the books of the Maya were burned
like the ones of Australia and the close North.

We can weep over such things
as lost love, as the passing away of others,
but also remember those birds, the bison,
the grief they have felt, and how the land hurts
in more chambers than one small heart
could ever hold.

Ceremony for the Seeds

These are the egg-shaped gourds
from the old homes
of our people a thousand years ago
and they are in my hand.
First, I introduce myself, the child
of the child of the old ones.
I listen to where they wish to live,
ask them about the birds they need,
the butterflies, insects when they blossom,
and sing them the songs
people say are forgotten,
the words for placing them in earth.
I promise to protect them
and paint the house as the old ones did
with the flowers, plants, even lizards,
birds and vines,
and I know, yes, there is renewal,
because this is what the seeds ask of us
with their own songs
when we listen to their small bundle of creation,
of a future rising from the ground,
climbing the fence.

The Radiant Field

Planting the pastures
this year by hand,
I put down dry leaves on top of seed
I've raked into earth,
put down straw
to fields with hope.

A History of Kindness

When a child becomes an animal in clouds
changing forms to other creatures,
our grief has become a kindness to the sky.

When the hay is baled and you worry, what if
a mouse or snake was inside,
that is a gentleness.

When the horses are fed and all that's left is a withered apple
for a woman to eat, and she is grateful
for the life of all things so she feeds it to the horse,
that is a good heart.

When you are gentle to the skin of others,
touching them softly, speaking with gentle words,
it is compassion.

When there is agreement among those
who might have argued instead,
it is a gift to all.

When skin is the first organ to form in the body of a woman,
and skin is the largest organ we have,
that is a mother's first protection.

If you still love the invisible place where a child once stood,
the heart recalling her soft hair, her long dark legs,
that is the spaciousness of memory.

And when you pick up the old woman on the worn road
to help her home and you see that inside
she has nothing, you give her the food you have.

You give the only can of coffee, then start her woodstove
and leave your coat behind on purpose.
What else would a real human do?

Remember

Remember your happiest days.
Then think of the life they carried you to.
They might have turned you inside out.
Consider Jonah, so tired of being a prophet,
royalty, he escaped
an ordinary man and took to the sea.

With joy one night, he watched lighted stars
break down one after another over dark sky water
just as the other men on board that ship
grew superstitious and threw him to the ocean.

Even in death water
a great journey waited
and when he didn't expect to live,
some great mouth opened and took him in
to a wondrous escape.

You never know when something, man, storm,
sea creature, a great wind of the sky
might take you to some other shore,
cough you up and drop you down
on new land, into a new story.
Once you were a prophet king.
Now you wear sackcloth and ash.

It is a hot country, the sun bearing down.
One night out of pity
a gourd grows tall to shade you.
It says if you care for me,
if you are kind enough to keep me alive
you will be sheltered by my shade.

Saved by a whale, saved by a gourd,
all to remind us again
just to be kind.

Sweet Silence

Each day a young man climbed the great wall.
He slipped through narrow streets of the city
between the world divided
by that of another.

Each day he gave the girl a neatly folded
story he wrote, one he'd just heard
about how a man made a monkey addicted
to sugar
in order to use sweetness to catch it.

The boy was too young to know it was a terrible story,
but one day he wrote that he would marry her.
Their children would be beautiful, as she was
and at the local playground they could hang by their knees
and climb ladders to blue sky.
By then the great wall would be gone
and they would have freedom.

But until that time he continued to climb west
to give her a perfectly folded story.
Until the day three large men took his thin arms
behind his back
and vanished him.

It was not uncommon for men to disappear,
but unlike some, he would never tell the story
of how they hung him naked from his wrists,
then burned his testicles,
all while he tried to remember the story
still somewhere in his shirt pocket.
He was just a boy
and even with the great blinding light on his face
he knew nothing
except that pain was a constant visitor.

Later, raw like others before him
from the rough floor, he wrote on the walls.

He wrote beautiful poetry about love
never true stories of what could happen to a human.
In code, he wrote how to tell families
where their sons were.

He wrote for the day
someone might take truth with them,
but for her he saved the finest, saying,
Every day
we were given the best.

Every day they gave us sugar.

Honey. My Friend

In our secret place,
the arch of red stone above us,
the bees live with their golden honey
sometimes trickling down the stone like liquid amber.
We think we are the only ones who know this place
and we watch the language of dance
composed by the light of sun
and sometimes find symmetries of wax on the ground,
or the dead sent out their eastern door
from a ceremonial world of light.

Their choreography of sun, the journeys still in time
remind me of the botanist who lived with our people
centuries ago, his journal rolled watertight in leather.
By following the plants
he found those of us who lived by them
and knew their uses.

We were the ones they called *People of the Sun*.

One night, he wrote, each person in a circle around the fire
told their story. Each sang or acted a story from their life,
the children making the elders laugh,
the men showing their powerful skills,
and then came the woman who danced her story.
Through her body she danced
the death of her husband and son by another tribe
that held her enslaved and more, her body said,
until she found her way home. This story was held
in her body and the sun brought her home,
a life so touching, everyone wept.

Why I think this today watching the bees above us
might be that the people were camped
against such stone that night long ago,
or it might be that each human doesn't know
their body tells its story and I read them,

but I think it is how he was so moved,
the sweetness of his grief for a woman
he never knew.

Hundreds of years have passed
but I think all this
as we stand here to watch once again
the bees arrive and leave,
the dance to make something
of one thing to another
and the dear friend, from his own nation
knows to take my hand.

Sunshine

The song of the sun is so loud my sweet cat hears it.
She is blind and I sing
to bring her to me.
Oh beautiful girl, Sunshine her name,
from the first morning
she woke after I found her,
when the dead fleas fell all around us,
I saw her
feral face and said,
Good morning, Sunshine.
Here is a song for you.
Oh beautiful, come to me, with your soft fervent
rumble, your little paws, still small, not like the others
who use them to reach out for food
steal from the table.
Come to me, dear one
I will sing for you all day
and in our own language;
English isn't enough for us
I know.
Sleep on my heart
now that you no longer sleep in the alley.
Dear cat, you who doesn't see the mouse dash by
but you hear the frogs, follow the sounds
and curl like a baby
wrapped in the bushes,

how like Moses
only following, not leading,
following the song
of my own body,
my legs, how you love the place between them
above the blanket on my chest,
how you love the spot between the breasts and lay
your head there as I sing to you,
Chi ma kina hey oh lina, ma cha kani okcha.
Mahli tamacheena saya lina tok.
Chanaschi, anko'ni soba, ofatiina'na che,
almost like my own language
but moved around for your ears,
and you come to me,
Sunshine,
like the warm ray in the window you love.

Some New Marvel

It isn't the warm water lake we swam,
half-afraid of catfish so large they could take down a calf.

Or the white eye of my uncle, so like a pearl.
Or the one with phantom pain after the war.

Once I wondered how the missing could cause pain.
Now I can understand the dynamic at work.

It was a reunion, my uncles together and all of them played
the fiddle, the guitar, mandolin, and other music.

We all danced together, laughing. For some that might be marvel enough.
Then one year of reunions came an uncle I'd never met.

They said he was *not right* after the war,
as if all the others were.

He lived at the VA hospital so long that he worked in the office.
I saw him and knew he was the one who came back right.

While the others hid shadows and foxholes in Japan or Germany
beneath all their moments of silence, his eyes were the kindest

eyes I'd ever seen. Compassion, they said. He was gentled
like a once wild horse in our world of the civil wild.

I was moved to love him because he had so much inside
and love was the word in my world those days.

It was some marvel that we were all together,
happy, and at night when we sat on grandma's porch

in the hot and humid dark Oklahoma night,
it smelled of summer earth, with fireflies and frogs.

We took turns churning the cream as the bag of ice melted
until we needed a grown man to come turn the handle.

It was so sweet, feeling rich as we did together,
almost straight of body, all of us almost whole.

Isn't It Love

Isn't it love that pulls me into the world,
the morning sky colored by rouge and becoming
deep and clear blue, as though a spring of water has entered
red earth? That is the place our relatives said the buffalo went
to wait for some safe day so their spirits could return.

Isn't it love that brings me to rise early to feed the horses their hay,
to clean the burro who sleeps in a pile of shavings
with the horse watching over her
in the manger, so young and surprised at the sounds she can make?
The horse is more silent. She is always the first
to receive, before the small burro she looks after.

But isn't it love that brings me to carrying grain, hay,
cleaning the water
when some days I would like to sit with the trees and a book
or paper and ink,
or look down to the field where deer and turkey
roam, where some trees are now down on their sides after the flood
came through and took away so much of the world?

When the old man told me it could happen, it was hard to believe
such a small creek might rise up and rage that way
but it became a river. Now I watch what will happen next spring
as this world is changed
and see what comes from that water.

Then, what can I call it at night when I open the wine
for a glass with my simple meal, so all alone without a heart
to beat against mine, or a hand to caress this body
so I think of the overflowing love of a solitude
that speaks so gently with myself,
then I caress the cat, brush the dog, take night hay to the horses
along with their sweet for the night.

The Writing of Snow

Snow is a book of history
writing its new language,
changed moment by moment,
but I read the tracks I find before the wind.
Here a flatness passes through
with claw marks on each side,
the tail of a beaver that slipped into the water
that wishes not to be petrified as ice
so the currents turn it crystal instead,
ice in beautiful turrets,
formations of geology,
layered, some old, some deep.

The story is newly changed
each day as I come read the tracks of the living,
bobcat, deer prints like punctuation,
and wonder, like the mysteries in a human,
what creatures, what songs, what countries,
swim beneath it all, or above
and the sky entire white
sometimes the wing marks on
new snow, each small crystal falling
with its own original say.

The Long Clouds

In a rare occurrence,
some miraculous spirit arrived,
born like the rest of the poor,
with only dirty water
to drink, to bathe, to cook.
That child woman dreamed
new bends and curves in the river's way.
She planted trees,
knowing they would clean water.
With her generous soul, she offered
the many gods of water anything they might need.
Now is the song of frogs,
the rising fireflies,
long-legged water walkers crossing over,
tadpoles growing legs.

The water snake curves a way through its domain,
even wells and cenotes,
new springs and rivers
return from beneath ground.

Once I swam through one of these
beneath the earth, inside another element.
At times clear light came from above
into the blue world that nurtures
the curve of this earth
returning to itself, like the rainbow
serpent holding itself
if only it was allowed.

Called down by trees,
fallen through the leaves of rainforest
back to earth,
pulled up through roots,
up through the canopy
are long clouds of the world,
long clouds becoming water
to be carried over the dunes.

How we all want love,
even the waters,
so let them be healthy and clean,
let us be carried
alive on the water of a planet,
along with it,
not just by it, but for it.

War Story: Heard

Do you ever think about where they are going,
the people you have to dispatch, ever look at their faces,
or the boys you take from homes?
It's so bad you think the world is going to end.
It's a warning to keep on with this job
and you have to think
it's not so bad. It's not wrong
to be afraid. To know it is to be alive.

Fences

I will never think of them in the same way
watching this woman with her brown skirt
throw her own body against the fence,
trying to climb.
Believing in freedom
she hits it like the wind
and still it keeps her
from the water of another life,
the dream of another imagined world
until finally she does nothing but, with all her might,
she throws a rock over it
so something reaches that destination.

What about the meek, the wretched,
the tired, the poor and yearning, the vulnerable
ones in their countries of life thieves
who, like the vigilantes,
have no fiber of mercy, no humanity
that has ever lived to be free,
no hunger or pain about them,
not for the fragile being of any child.
They forget they were the land thieves,
the takers, the soldier gangs.
Like their poor dogs
they will find some other bone
to crack, some gristle,
some other nerve of mercy
for the penned, fenced people
like birds with wings of beauty
locked in a small cage
in a room with windows
to the desired world.

Tulsa

1.

Not the white men riots of the past,
but only yesterday
a man was shot in the back by a police officer.
She was white, he black, she a medic
who didn't help him, nor did the others who arrived.
For minutes they watched while they could have
saved him but for his skin.
I try to imagine watching a man die
because they fear or hate the darkness
of a human, a man who had no weapon, not even words,
the man who began his day like any other,
saying to his wife, Helene, I'll be back early today.
I'm taking you out for Mother's Day.
She sat under the lamp with her tea,
finishing the hem of their daughter's jeans
before she left for work. The pictures on the table
of their children, children with more and less melanin
in their skin. They are beautiful and smart, loved,
and doesn't it scare a father that they are learning to drive?
Does it scare you that one dates a white boy and they might love?
What does the officer think
as she stands, watching the man lose blood and die?
That she might get in trouble? That she won't?

2.

I am a dark woman. Dark. Darker. Even Darker.
A Chickasaw woman from the very old days,
but if the police saw me today they would think me white,
maybe whiter than them. I can pass.
They would save me, not knowing
the history in my skin
that lies to them
and how I might be thinking of them with fear
or something worse.

3.

The kids from the tribe had a chance
to go to a soccer game, so they kept up their grades;
the game was their reward. Excited, they rode the bus, so quiet,
and sat on the bleachers, learning the game, watching,
until the white men above them poured beer
on the children's color of skin, poured beer on their coats
from the unknown reservation world
from which they came.
White Men.
Native Children.
I wonder, if like the policewoman,
their soul came from some other place.

All Angels in the Dark

Before the wars
my mother and father danced.
He flew her about.
She was pure energy and grace
to his young strength and life.
Then their world disappeared into the war.

Some days I sat on the closet floor
beneath my mother's clothing,
all soft cloth, exotic to touch,
dresses scented with her perfume
and footwear with open-toed shoes
patent leather and suede.

Some nights grown-ups were inside talking
with beer or whiskey.
We hid under trees
in our nightclothes, fresh with bath soap,
hair braided tight and clean,
cousins of our America,
we had the smell of the great pine,
fresh grasses, earth
and our own shadows of immensity
from the porch light,
our innocence
with the recollected scent of wildflowers,
petals soft as my mother's dresses.

In all our dark hiding places,
you'd think we'd be the ones
to grow wings and vanish
like her dresses I adored
and all our missing fathers.

Peeling an Apple

After two wars
my father knew
eternity.
Peeling the apple,
red skin from sweet fruit
he pared slowly
such elegant work
to cut without error
a single loop
of red flesh,
all of it
flayed
this
one
long
skin.

Other apples sat inside the bowl,
still whole, the year's good crop,
and I'd think of all the curling skin
winding deeply, kindly,
carefully held
around us, being twirled
into the infinite
finite.

Book Four

The Other Country

The Night in Turkey

I forget many things
but I will never forget the dancers that night
in the stone church out far in the country.
It was dark. The milk in the cold sky
was strongly drawn.
Inside we sat with tea
and the men came out,
nodded at one another.
They were just men
in white robes
and it seems music began
but I can barely remember
because the men began encircling themselves
at the very core of life
and whirling. They stepped in together,
their robes opening out
like tender flowers in first spring.

It seemed even the sky unfurled
in all its starlit splendor,
one white moon in the darkness
after another
and the world began to warm again
the stones of the church
as we were entranced
and something inside us, all this
human was silenced and dancers opened
something greater in the darkness
and we were there with them,

we were one of them,
we were in a world that bloomed one winter night
from inside the dark building of stones
that fell away from us.

The Camel

Last night the camel
on its knobby long legs nearby,
so surprisingly gentle
laid itself on earth,
dust rising up, sand in his hair,
all awkward grace,
not the most loved creature of them all,
but there it was, smelling of plants
I can't name,
and then it laid its head so gently on my leg,
so warm it was,
such a sudden act of kindness.

In the Great Desert

Apple, I call you food
not the red green beauty you are.

Erg, I call you desert dune
that came to cover this place
in just one night of wind.
Last night.

I stayed safe from the sound
of the great covering of sand
with this little teapot,
brewing for friends.

An apple is grace in the desert.
Still my shoulder hurts,
I carried inside a lamb and then an injured bird,
then my own heart lying there
heavy and broken with all the rest.

Heart, can you remember
this, the constant way of the inconstant desert
and remember the white camel
born just after the storm
gentle as a human touch
after bringing the infant and mother inside
as well we must for any future,
gentle as the human touch
and it caressing me back, nuzzling my hand
in that fur, coarse and soft
beneath the roughness
and I gave her mother the apple,
everything I had left.

Home on the Island

We pass homes with red tile roofs,
clothes drying on lines
and a tree with fallen oranges where I bend
to pick up the ground-tumbled fruits.

The wind in this country is magic
with its history as the element
that drove men to the seas, lost
on islands, and if they found home,
they left it again.

That's when I see the house on the island,
alone in its water wilderness
of the unseen beneath, unknown fishes swimming
and dolphins farther out, here long-legged birds
and a cat fishing with paws at the edge.

I could call it home,
this tiny island in the wind.
Perhaps it is the evergreens or black stone,
the walkway of wooden sticks
that seem afloat from here to there
in the wind-curling water.

I ask my friend, Could you live on the sea that way?
He says, It's wonderful.
Maybe I will meet Circe one day.
I think, What about the singing at the loom
and the men who were transformed?

But beneath this walk,
the fish, the small octopus.
You know I can't help
but feel
something that alive inside.
All my lives could be here.

Sky Above a Crumbling World

Sunrise

The sky is already deep blue,
clouds of water in their constant
changing, throwing down shadows
on the ground of all beings,
the small with claws, teeth,
the large with fur,
walking on four paws,
and those leaping from clear water
already becoming another creature,
all the dying and living
people without homes, desolate
from the desert, from chemicals,
broken buildings, but still
the beautiful children
are playing, not aware
anything forever changed,
seeds can no longer multiply.
And yet the sun rising and falling
as always looks down on us,
all that has been taken.
And still the sky so beautifully deep,
clouds so constantly changing.
The fluid language of the past
still crosses above the world,
and an ancient ocean
dwells around each sacred land,
each now with fallen blood,
because whenever in time has there been peace?

Even the fallen clouds are on this land
as they move to other worlds,
as I wonder about peaceful times,
the cloud shadows on stones
cross the crumbling, the broken,
leaving homes of those other countries hated.
The men of belief
didn't care if a child
was the only possession some mother could carry
under the sky
with all the other walkers,
the design of a rug
still in her memory,
all else taken with a grenade
through the window of their lives.
Thank god when no one is home
but even so all shadows cross this sky with fear.

River Singing

We rained from the water of our mothers,
born to the river passages of each life.
We grew up from the cradle of a river,
the sweetness of the taste of spring when rains arrive
and the river enters trees in the first turn of green,
our lifeblood traveling
to the unknown bends of tomorrow.

Tributaries, arteries, veins,
we are the river, sometimes weeping,
sometimes laughing
in this brief life
and we can't help it but we love other waters,
opening glorious into one another.

The world, the waterways we are
travel in ways you can't tell from others.

The heart of earth beats gently,
but the song of a river is carried
even under the ground,
its own heart set on great ocean waters.
Some days I wonder how anyone is content
on plains, on mountains, but then
doesn't water live everywhere
beneath our feet
as it journeys from one holy site to another?

Book Five

The Current Veins

The Kill

One morning the dog barked.
We live in wilderness
so it is not unusual except he didn't stop.
I was in the house
combing my hair, typing,
preparing for work.
When I went to feed the horses,
outside was blood,
blood on the snow.
I touched each part of their bodies,
their feral legs,
each wild neck, artery beating,
chest, bellies well-fed,
then finally followed the red map on snow
through wind blowing cold and sharp,
covering the tracks
but revealing the red,
as I followed blood toward the fence
and climbed through,
by then just a few spots
and then all the visible bones
just a short while ago running alive across the ravine
with flesh on them.

And the kill, the deer without hooves
to kick any longer at pain.
I can't know if fear overtook it,
but I have seen the pack of wolves,
five ghostly presences
passing on the other hill,
soft in the snow,
careful and slow
and here was the deer,
now only bone
with pink scrapes of teeth
cut into bone,
nothing else. The snow wind
had blown their tracks away
but it all started only moments before
their handsome feast.

The Bears Eating

The ocean is never still.
The earth moves. We know
because there are those who measure it.
Nothing is ever quiet.
No living thing is silent.
The cracking of bones wakes me at night
and I do not know this new sound,
but two bears are at the skeleton wolves left behind,
eating the fat in bones.
Even last winter's old death makes a noise
with the new life roused.

Burying the Horse

She came to me
mere bone
dark,
blood in hooves,
barely able
to move or eat
without help.
All the way home
she watched me
behind the trailer
and that was a
beginning
of what would become
the long black hair
in the wind,
the looking back to see
that I was
still there,
my own hair black then
blowing as I leaned out
so she could see my face.

In time
she grew red
and larger,
never real big
but turned out
to be an Arabian
and one day
I saw her healthy,
running like wind

was pushing her along
its currents.

All the years after
she was grateful for every morsel
of food and for grass.
How she loved it,
and the dog
pretending to be a horse
out in the field bent over
as if eating beside her.

She was the one not to ride
because she'd been so abused
nothing could make her turn
from grass
or walk on.
Nothing.

And so the years went,
senior feed,
medicine feed,
love. To all she showed
such gratitude
and care returning
as if to a barn
and her eyes showed
the happy fragility
and kindness.

That same look
when I stayed
with her head in my lap
as she was dying.
I held the red umbrella
over her from the Oklahoma
summer heat
as we waited
four hours for the death-maker
to arrive
and put her down
then leave me in the chosen place
with her lifeless body
while her sister
studied her
and understood
she was gone
and she was alone,

and she stayed while I waited
for the backhoe
to arrive then
dig a hole
and I wrapped her
in more than my arms,
in an Indian blanket,
the design of wind,

and began trying to get her down
that hole.
A horse is a heavy thing
as I bent and pushed
with a friend and his one good arm,
and I felt wretched
as I saw how she finally landed
not the way I wanted
with her dignity
and fragile beauty,
but fell into the
consuming hole
which swallowed
her any way it wanted.

Oh my love,
how it hurt my body so
but even more my heart
to get you down there
with so little of the help
you'd always given me
just to see you eat
with such untethered happiness
and to see you run
across fields with wild
freedom,

to have watched you heal
from bones to belly
and part of me
is beneath that ground
in the blanket
wrapped and singing
a good horse song
the horse song
the horse song.
Each nation has them,
even the nation
of gone horses.

Haunting

We are the people from mangroves,
plants that create good earth, good water,
removing salt from the ocean
to make a sweet spring where small fish grow
with bountiful food.

Then we lived near cane fields,
the ones that stopped land
from falling into rivers.

From the deep past
we haunt you
with nothing more than a feeling
of what you are, the bloodshed
you created and survived.

With words from this country
we lived along the margins of worlds
and maybe you do not know
we are present in your daily moments,
a person so like you, just like you
but maybe stronger with our knowledge.
Imagine yourself as that life,
centuries of knowing this place
and the fine work of your own hands.

You felt something follow you,
the living person inside,
and you have heard this voice for years
like a bell, invisible as air,
clear as a gentle rain

in that delicate slippage
so like the skin, permeable,
a thin line between what you believe gone
and what is still present.

I recall my gentle father, content in his life,
his body so like mine
across from where I sit at the table,
with coffee of milk and sugar he made
for this child each morning
before he introduced me to the living past.

Just before he left his body
they came to him,
the women of our clan,
our house, the ancestral mothers
and he spoke all their names.

After he greeted them,
or asked the name again
or to pronounce it,
he said, This is my daughter and I love her.
It was a moment so holy
I had to ask if I could tell it
but yes, they need to know, they said.
We are still here
and someday I'll be the one speaking the names.

To Be Held

To be held
by the light
was what I wanted,
to be a tree drinking the rain,
no longer parched in this hot land.
To be roots in a tunnel growing
but also to be sheltering the inborn leaves
and the green slide of mineral
down the immense distances
into infinite comfort
and the land here, only clay,
still contains and consumes
the thirsty need
the way a tree always shelters the unborn life
and waits for the healing
after the storm
which has been our life.

Arctic Night, Lights Across the Sky

We are curved together,
body to body, cell to cell,
arm over another.
The world is this bed for the cold night,
one cat curled in the bend of a knee,
dog at the feet,
my hand in yours, we are embraced
in animal presence, warmth,
the sea outside sounding
winter waves, one arriving after another
from the mystery far out
where in the depths of the sea
are other beings
that create their own light,
this world all one heartbeat.

Dear Child

Yes, tragedies happen too often to explain
so I won't try. I will just write this for you.
When at this moment, the green ambition of spring
pushes earth away to let a tendril rise,
our tiny new tree finally breaks open the stone
above it. Overnight I see this miracle of what One
can do. If you were here,
that tree larger each year, I would love you still, and again
more each day until the whole of creation would open
to keep you from leaving. I would hold you tight
in my arms and my hands, and I know you
would be in these hands once again like water.

for Jayla

Absences

Who knows the deep tunnels of snakes
and that their dens near the spring
have been lived in a thousand generations?

They shed their skin so perfectly
even the eye remains in the body sleeve
with scale, rattle, reptilian odor,
all of a piece near the scraping stone.

Such absences remind me of how the missing
remains present,
my uncle's toes shot off,
his phantom pain
with no nerve or bone, no flesh
to back it up,
but still hurting.

I know what's gone
can aggrieve deep as the forest once here,
all the invisible creature life
still falling unseen
through deep leaves and branches downed,
the majestic endangered missing
the beautiful gone.

Absence is the missing presence
that travels everywhere at once.

One day my eyes were awake
and I have to tell you
I saw the spirit of my horse
and how she lived with herself
standing tall in the field,
then bent, eating
the ends of green grasses.
I hope it is true,
that we are never so far away
and the absent will remain
with us forever
even the remembered and loved child
that was taken away,
but when do we have something back?

Water Gods of the Next World

This is a time when I wonder if we did truly enter the fourth world
as they say, or if that time is yet to come, because we entered this world
    for peace.
I ask the man whose teachers are clouds; they live in caves and mountains.
They live in thick forests and some of them come out
    through broken windows
of houses made with round stones. Others come from the crashing waters
where seas converge, the Pacific and Atlantic with the Southern.
Cloud teachers and water sages wear white. Sometimes they live
with the world of birds. When they pass over this world, they see suffering
and they weep rain.

The good man tells me, If you climb the peaks, sometimes you hear
    them singing.
Clouds are people I don't know except they are mostly humble
crossing our sky. Still, I want to know if we have yet another realm to enter,
to emerge from our ways of living now, to climb a reed, or leave our
    crystal cave.
I thought the goddesses of clouds and gods of rain
were merely the breath of wind, but some are the story of storms
held back too long from telling they've seen how hard the world has grown.

In the beginning, before there were flower people, before bees,
    were birds and sky.
There was no land. Birds rested on water held by clouds.
For others, a miraculous spirit was born in the presence of animals,
like the rest of the poor with an earth but no clean water to drink.
Tree Woman arrived. She planted and rooted and changed the course
    of water
so life could go on without illness. For this they were grateful.

These are only a few of the stories and songs that exist. All are true.
In the dry land corn waits for the holy presence of clouds
and human beings dance barefoot on hot earth with their love
        for rustling corn.
Others live in the place where waters meet,
where the people climb mountains
with the deer to watch those clouds fly in, dark, full, ready to give birth,
and soon the water breaks and it flows.
Then those of the water clan know the songs that call water forth.
They place tobacco prayers on surging rivers where clouds rise
and see their prayers float on the water, then carry the songs
to greater waters.

Yet how I do wonder if one day we'll climb from this world
into the one of peace where countries do not harm their own,
where rumors do not end in war, leaders have wisdom and integrity,
caring for the free clean water of this world.
They know the stories of all people are true and respect them.
This is how I know we are not yet at the beginning of the world
as some of us were told.

Fawn

Outside the house, the doe
so carefully explores the grasses,

the brush beneath trees, the places others have bent
in sleep circled together

and the yearling stands nearby.
The legs of another almost invisible still inside,

wanting to enter the world, a mother looking for dangers.
I stop my own life

to watch the infant moving in her,
remembering the fawn that once needed help,

half dragged out the wrong way, the doe
left in that position

until she fell, exhausted enough to let me
reach for the rest.

But this time I merely watch this creation,
beautiful, even with ticks and insects, wounds and scrapes

that humans don't envision because our sight is not large
enough. But I remember it all

and my own daughter with her child inside the canal
before she was born

after the ocean fell
from between her legs like rain.

And for that single measure, some vision large enough
to encompass all the great terrain of the future.

This Morning

This morning the doe speaks to her young
outside the window.
I do not know what is said but listen,
their love is great as ours.
If the coyote comes the mothers chase it
hoping more are not behind the trees,
praying to the god of deer.

I Saw Them Dancing

They were not two males in a territorial battle,
but does lifting their legs and small hooves
before bowing to one another in respect ending their dance
then curling back down near each other around their young
in the long spring grasses.

I remember the bend in the road
when I carried my woven basket of branches
and saw the two does dance.

It was the season of trees blooming after a rain,
and in the ray of light, the last of day,
were other inhabitants
that carry only their beauty to shine this land.

It was the season when blue dragonflies
weave about all the other creatures,
the spiders drop down on elegant strands
they say are stronger than we can create.

Each life says to the other, Yes,
you are an animal, you are a song,
you are a runner, a flyer, you are so alive.

We were all created together
with this herd of twilight dancers, more than one.
Then they went into the tangle of thickets
this woman can never follow.

For the Women

A breeze moved the tall grasses in the field.
I know the bones and hollows of these meadows,
and think why not we
muscle to muscle
beauty to beauty
life to life
in the untangled spirit of herd
like the day when all I did was step round the bend
and see the dancers.

White Deer, Your Direction I Follow

From the pasture this morning,
out by the old tools,
from the white under-leaves of poplar shade,
I follow the deer
to the place she wishes to take me,
the trail beyond men with rifles or bows.

The place we journey is far but
no pain creeps into my body.
This deer is the map
I have waited for.
She is something come here like the white dog
my people followed to and across
the roaring river,
to the next world after this creation.

The white deer leaps the dirty river.
I follow in the wake of it,
the deer so like a cloud
I know she is more than a guide,
so perhaps she is partly
the way of milk, such sweetness,
the mothering sky,
the great countenance of spiral, of animals
from our earth, the milk of forever
an infant will seek.

Or is she merely a small deer
curled inside herself,
a spiral of innards, always content
for the suckling,
such a creation,
I almost forget the path,
to follow.

In these words I am almost lost
from the trail
so simply it could disappear
from the body journey
with too much wonder,
when the deer becomes smoke,
merely an animal of light
passing now into the wilderness
or rising with the prayer,
the human words

right here, right now,
you have to ask,
how often do you see it,
how often does it come to you,
how often, really,
do you follow?

Grace

Waking on the edge of morning, still dark,
the owl speaks one last word,
and I hear this world
from the other side of daylight
and go to sit at water,
with great knowledge
of the eloquent speeches
water makes, watching for the trout
in the next uplift from water,
and hear the insects,
their music great as any,
meaningful as frogs before a rain.

Then it comes, gentle rain.
That is what makes for grace
and I can believe in such softness.
None of the miseries of the world are meant for me,
not this morning.
If you ask each day, it will tell you that
the continent is moist
with multitudes of life
beginning every moment.

While others gather their pieces of hurt,
to tell their stories,
I try to remember, none were meant for me,
not this morning,
not war, loss, death, not pain.
In that first edge of morning,

let's embrace the birds, the air, the once again
world as it grows in this manner
and, like us all, needs embraced
for everything that has been hurt.

Here Is

Here is to the waters,
to the great fish that live inside, to the plankton,
the forests of golden kelp,
a flying squid that passes over great ships,
also the great one that glides beneath those ships,
the whale that rises up, something like joy,
the humpback songs we heard from under our small canoe,
and to the great river artery of the continent,
the large gar who shields the mussels
with their own story hidden,
the round shining pearls
inside a safe and homely shell
of protection.

The Current Veins of History

are open
as worlds and borders redefine
themselves.

We wish for some new seed of vision
so the world may grow if only for a moment
silent, wordless, and fresh
as a bare room with windows open.

Friend,
even you I may never know,
none of us alike,
we are all in the same
rushing current of life,
each with our one-celled beginning
primordial life opening
to step out toward years of life
with stories of those who birthed us,
we hope flowing with love
even with childhoods of hurt
from being human,
and for a time it seems all fine.

In this moment of stopping
in the room safe with curtains billowing,
for just this moment can't we touch one another
and ask about our lives?

Even the earth knows these veins
that run like rivers
of sweet water into countries
great one day, gone the next,
or flowing into one
another to create something new.

As we are silent in this moment, to be a friend,
no weapon, not even arrows of words,
just easy human waters together.
Be like the animal that opens hardness
and carries inside a pearl or a goddess
that steps out to a new human accord.

Author's Note and Ackowledgments

Some of these poems contain the history, astronomy, geography, and mythology of my own Chickasaw people who survived numerous wars against them since their peaceful early 1500s. They were attacked long before nations in the Southwest and Northwest were even known and mentioned by the ethnographers. Some of this work also contains historical information pertinent to the rest of my family, all Oglala Lakota.

During my time as the writer for my Chickasaw Nation, I not only taught and wrote a novel and *Dark. Sweet: New and Selected* but devoted much time and attention to our past, noting materials usually ignored by historians and archaeologists, works that might have seemed insignificant to others: journals in botany, paleobotany, our enslavement in Barbados, and the writings of early invaders and others.

Still, these poems are personal, even if they contain our new historiography like that appearing with so many other tribal nations in our time. This is all a significant part of who I am, what I am, all being the people, place, and ecosystems of my origins.

Poetry is a form of magic for me. Never did I have opportunities for studies in literature or even for an education. I knew no one who went to a university or college. The first educated, influential person I met was my cousin in California where I worked as a nurse's aid and a dental assistant. It was long after my graduation from high school.

My cousin, Sakej Henderson, is now head of the Native Law Centre in Saskatoon, Canada, his partner a prominent indigenous educator, Marie Battiste (MiqMaw.) He inspired me to night classes, then to Junior College, a commuter school, and, after discovering a first book of contemporary poetry, I asked to attend classes at the University of Maryland while working as a teacher's aide with handicapped children.

I am grateful to friends mentioned later, who offered wonderful conversations and deep, lasting friendships.

I am also grateful to financial support from the Native Arts and Culture Foundation, the Lannan Foundation, Helen Foundation, the significant PEN Thoreau Award, and others received before this book began.

Mostly, I am indebted to my ancestors. They offer me this language, and poetry is the strongest of my first languages. They survived terrible hardships so that I might live today when none of us were meant to survive. I owe them these works, these words, and heartfelt acknowledgments. I offer them my love. Thank you, my people, for the beauty of these poems, this opportunity to live.

This work is for the Water Protectors, attacked by private, hired armies, particularly for the elders injured and traumatized in dog cages by the North Dakota Law Enforcement employees.

My gratitude is richly given to my many readers throughout the world. You have changed my life. Your letters and forums, discussions and academic panels about my work has been a gift to me. The life of a poet is not a life of wealth. As my friend Pamela Uschuk says, Poetry is work that keeps you humble. This life of mine may be humble, but is rich in love, trees, and waters. I thank you all from my heart.

Without many friends and places, these poems may not have come together into this book. I thank Mesa Refuge and the board for their generosity of space and time to work on writings. Gratitude to Rowen White, with me there, for the generosity of her slow cooking, and to the Cultural Conservancy and Melissa Nelson for the wonderful visit. And to dancing woman for the oil to help heal my badly scarred face.

I thank dear friends Marilyn Auer and Kathleen Cain for their movie and coffee dates at the time these poems were being revised, and friends Debra Jang and Ricardo Salas, always here to heavy lift even my heart. I have much thanks to Karen Oser for my occasional days off of outdoor labor so I could write while she took over the horse girls and manure loading for me. I miss your presence, Karen.

For Helene Atwan and Hayley Lynch, for your patience, friendship, and work.

Thank you to the late Janice Gould and to Mimi Wheatwind for conversations and letting me dance through the house, and to neighbors Chris and Ciara for occasional meals out, and for helping with my great large snowdrifts down in this hidden world. And to David and Rita to the near west, for clearing snow at the top without even telling. This gratitude includes the Chickasaw community here, especially Stephen and Lisa Bingham, and Carol Berry. Here I must add my poet cousin Becky Travis, Ed Travis, and Doris (my closest blood animal sister) McAtee, still near our Oklahoma country, Doris still with memory of our one first Old Mother.

With unimaginable gratitude to Amanda Wheeler for the healing she offers. Without her there would be no work. And to Craig Fiorno for the needles stitching life together. And Lonnie Granston, marathon man, for appreciating my quotes.

With much happiness that Joe and Becky Hogan call enthusiastically for great book conversations. And for the times my brother, photographer Larry Henderson, and my sister, Donna Henderson, visit with me, as well as my far sister, Anna Mae Henderson. Incredible love and thanks to my cousin Sakej Henderson, who showed me there were many paths. Family is important, even so far away, as is my daughter Tanya Thunder Horse, my grandchildren Cami and Danielle Griffith, and my great grandchildren, Jayla Rodriguez, no longer embodied, and for the amazingly vibrant and alive, loving little ones, Kyan Red Star, and Kayse Red Star.

I am in love with this land, the animals, all the growing life and the water passing through here, with the trees speaking in the wind outside the windows, the horse girls, the two inside cats and sweetheart of a dog. Thank you, Home, Land, Soil, Trees, and History.

Thanks, finally, but not least, all you Torrey House women working for the voices of the land. I'm sure there are many at the press I haven't met, but Rachel, Anne, Kathleen, and Kirsten, you have been wonderful. Your enthusiasm has carried this book on a wave of beauty and I have great hopes for it.

Thank you, David Curtis, for giving me time, movies, and loving friendship. You have helped more than you can know.

Old Mother, I look forward to more life together.

—Linda Hogan, *Koihouma*, Chickasaw
Old Turtle Clan

About the Author

Linda Hogan (Chickasaw) is an internationally recognized author and speaker. Her novel *Mean Spirit* was a finalist for the Pulitzer Prize, and her poetry collection *The Book of Medicines* was a National Book Critics Circle Award finalist. Her most recent book of poetry is *Dark. Sweet: New and Selected Poems*. Her novels include *People of the Whale, Solar Storms*, and *Power*. Essay collections include *Dwellings: A Spiritual History of the Living World* and *The Radiant Lives of Animals*. Hogan's work explores human relationships with the environment, Indigenous science, and traditional knowledge. She has received a Guggenheim Fellowship, a National Endowment for the Arts Fellowship, a Lannan Fellowship, a Native Arts and Culture Fellowship, a PEN Thoreau Award, and numerous other recognitions.

Torrey House Press

Voices for the Land

The economy is a wholly owned subsidiary of the environment, not the other way around.

—Senator Gaylord Nelson, founder of Earth Day

Torrey House Press is an independent nonprofit publisher promoting environmental conservation through literature. We believe that culture is changed through conversation and that lively, contemporary literature is the cutting edge of social change. We strive to identify exceptional writers, nurture their work, and engage the widest possible audience; to publish diverse voices with transformative stories that illuminate important facets of our ever-changing planet; to develop literary resources for the conservation movement, educating and entertaining readers, inspiring action.

Visit www.torreyhouse.org for reading group discussion guides, author interviews, and more.

As a 501(c)(3) nonprofit publisher, our work is made possible by the generous donations of readers like you.

Torrey House Press is supported by the National Endowment for the Arts, Back of Beyond Books, The King's English Bookshop, Wasatch Global, Jeff and Heather Adams, Stephen Strom, Diana Allison, Kirtly Parker Jones, Kitty Swenson, Jerome Cooney and Laura Storjohann, Heidi Dexter and David Gens, Robert Aagard and Camille Bailey Aagard, Kathleen and Peter Metcalf, Rose Chilcoat and Mark Franklin, Stirling Adams and Kif Augustine, Charlie Quimby and Susan Cushman, Doug and Donaree Neville, the Barker Foundation, the Sam and Diane Stewart Family Foundation, the Jeffrey S. and Helen H. Cardon Foundation, Utah Division of Arts & Museums, and Salt Lake County Zoo, Arts & Parks. Our thanks to individual donors, subscribers, and the Torrey House Press board of directors for their valued support.

Join the Torrey House Press family and give today at
www.torreyhouse.org/give.